Money is A Gift

By Harmony Rowell

DEDICATION

This book is dedicated to my magnificent parents and fabulous friends and family. I am grateful and appreciative for you all.

Acknowledgements

First and foremost, I want to thank my Lord and Savior Jesus Christ because without him this wouldn't be possible. I want to thank my mom, for believing in me and always pushing me to greatness. My Family and friends who always believed in me, supported me and saw my potential. I want to thank all who helped with creating my book.

Remember that:

Money will always match your mindset

-Joe Vitale

As a young child, I remember telling my mother, "Go to the machine, press the buttons and get the money out."

My mom replied by saying, "Pumpkin, it doesn't work like that, you have to have money in the account to take it out."

ATM

My mom always told me that money was a gift. My mom explained to me that money is earned in many different ways. She told me there are 4 things you can do once you earn money. The first is to SAVE your money. It is important to save money. Saving is very important because you should always save for all the things you need. The second is to TITHE. Tithing is when you give 10% of your money consistently to a church or sanctuary. Some people donate to charities or places to help people in need. The third is to INVEST your money. Investing is when you save money to get a percentage or profit on the money. For example, if I invested $20 and earned 50% of the $20, I would have earned $10, so now I would have $30 instead of $20. Last but not least is to SPEND your money. We all have to spend money and buy things we need or want.

B
A
C

Monday, my mom and I went to one of our favorite stores. My mom always bought tons of stuff when we went to the store. The deal was, if I behaved I could "window shop" in the toy section. Today, I was on my best behavior. We went to the toy section. I saw so many toys, dolls, slime, games and books. I love to read!

I asked my mom if I could get a doll, Mom replied, "Sweetheart, we are window shopping."

I asked, "What is window shopping?" "Window shopping is when you look at things, but don't buy them."

"Aah-man!" I shouted.

Mom said, "Remember, money is a gift and you have to earn it." Instead of buying a toy, my mom bought a rewards board. I was excited to get my rewards board.

When we got home we set up my rewards board. Mom said money is a gift and I can earn my own allowance by behaving and doing chores. I was so excited about this opportunity. Now I can buy things I need and want with my own money.

By Saturday, I earned $25. I was well behaved in school, as usual. I kept my room clean and I did ALL of my chores. I worked so hard to earn my gift............ Money. With the $25, I saved $10 in my piggybank and tithed $2.50 during church. The rest I decided to spend.

Sunday evening, Mom and I went to the store. I purchased a doll with the money I had left. I was so excited. My mother taught me the most valuable lesson about money.

Money is earned and money is a gift.

CASHIER

ABOUT THE AUTHOR

Harmony L. Rowell is a seven-year-old author and entrepreneur. Harmony lives in Boston, MA with her mother and dog Libby. Harmony loves her parents. Harmony loves to read and go to school. Harmony loves gymnastics, dancing and spending time with friends and family in her spare time. Harmony aspires to be a vet because she loves animals.

CPSIA information can be obtained
at www.ICGtesting.com
Printed in the USA
BVHW021258230721
612716BV00007B/235

* 9 7 8 1 7 3 6 8 0 9 8 1 5 *